Relationship Research Institute of Michigan
801 Broadway Avenue, NW
Suite 443
Grand Rapids, Michigan 49504

ISBN: 9798638073091

2nd Edition, First Printing, 2013

Table of Contents

Introduction

Rationale of our Mission: How we intend to help couples help themselves

- Why we are concerned with "resiliency"

- How others recommend that you use
  this book

    - The *Relationship Resiliency Assessment*

Chapter One: Preserving and Enhancing our We-ness (Cohesion)

- What resiliency "we-ness" is
- Discovering your own we-ness
- "Catastrophic thinking"
- Baggage
- Space for your relationship
- "Life after birth!"
- Go take a hike (together)!
- Stress is the way of life; The difficulty often lies in how we handle the change involved in life's transitions

Chapter Two: Preserving and Enhancing our Problem-Solving Communication

- Confusion and disagreement are *opportunities!*
- Good fortune comes from:
    - Plans for problem-solving
    - Realistic goals
    - Partners who collaborate

- Assessing your problem-solving resources

- Keeping your lives reasonable, simple, and do-able

- Common barriers to decision-making
- *You can create your good luck!*

    - Unrecognized clash of coping styles
    - Thinking in terms of extremes
    - Catastrophic thinking
    - A sense of "impossibility"
    - Parental legacies
- Good fortune comes from:
    - Plans for problem-solving
    - Realistic goals
    - Partners who collaborate

- Assessing your problem-solving resources

- Keeping your lives reasonable, simple, and do-able

- Common barriers to decision-making
- *You can create your good luck!*

    - Unrecognized clash of coping styles
        - Thinking in terms of extremes
        - Catastrophic thinking
        - A sense of "impossibility"
        - Parental legacies

Chapter Three: Creating and Maintaining and Organized Adaptive Approach

- "Growing stronger, together" - A three-legged stool
    1. WE-ness
    2. Open interchange
    3. Organized approach

- Assessing how organized we are

 **Talk to Us**

About the Author

Introduction

Why We Are Concerned with "Relationship Resiliency"

Over half of the couples we encounter have been on the verge of divorce. But if the two of you want to avoid the end of your relationship, you can get pain and stress relief within an hour. Your relationship will be affirmed as a "good thing," and you will start to become best friends and lovers again. *In this ebook you will find realistic hope for your future that may be eluding you right now.* Because its directions are based on scientifically-proven results.

For the past three decades celebrated marital counseling experts have observed that counseling that is focussed on what is wrong in a relationship is destructive. It enhances and confirms bad feelings and ends with a breakup. Why? *"You don't need to rehash (and rehearse) what you are doing wrong in relationships. You need to recognize what you are doing right!"*

Relationship Resiliency trumps all other relationship variables. Most researchers and people focus on relationship satisfaction and happiness, or they look at factors involved in relationship break-up. However, common sense tells us we cannot be happy together all the time. We all have unique traits. Our partners may like many of our traits; other traits, not so much. We feel the same about our partners. Also, we tend to see things more negatively when our moods are down and we are feeling irritable. At such negative times we may tend to be pessimistic and focus on our partners' negative traits or on our 'problems.'

Let's face it. In the beginning relationships are typically *recreational*. We are falling in love and really enjoy being together. However, over time relationships acquire an additional purpose: a partnership to help us handle the complexities of our communal life. And it does that! And we are reasonably happy and feel confident as long as the way we have learned to do things suits the way our life currently is. However, as our life changes — we commit to each other, and then move in together — things that possibly were not even noticeable before *suddenly are vital now*. For example, our personal habits (clothes on the floor, dishes in the sink), and how we each manage money, time, friends, and family. At times like this we become confused, tense, and irritable. But, once we change in order to adapt to our new situation, we settle in and feel good about ourselves once again. It's a predictable *cycle*.

This is why the Relationship Research Institute of Michigan is focused on resiliency. Moods may come and go, but the real payoff for the two of you is how well the two of you are able to take on all the different challenges of life together. As you read this ebook and practice the exercises, you will begin to increase your resilience which in turn will increase your ability to admire, respect, love and value your partner. Your self esteem as individuals and as a couple will become *realistically* positive. You will have evidence-based confidence in yourselves *("We can DO stuff!")* and order in your lives. You won't be tempted to turn your relationship future over to strangers with negative methods and their own ideas about what is wrong with you and needs to be "fixed".

This Elixir Called "Resiliency"

Social scientists have tried to draw attention to resiliency for the past five decades. It has been a tough sell: Traditional "mental health" has been defined in terms of what's *wrong* with individuals; not what is right about them. For example, "She is dependent," "He is hostile," or "She feels inadequate". There are three errors here:

1. All people may feel inept, sad, angry, or scared in some situations. They also feel confident, cheerful, and assertive in others. What appear to be someone's hard-wired "traits" depends on what is going on and when and where it is taking place.

2. Difficulty in life is unavoidable. There are certain changes in the *status quo* that make everyone anxious and to which every relationship must learn to adapt. For example, if you move in together, what happens? You now have to accommodate each other's living habits; move from recreational goals to problem-solving and a division of labor; deal more closely with other family members. And so on! And none of it is wrong; It just IS.

3. By finding "problems" in natural occurrences, and focusing on what people lack, everyone's attention is distracted from what is real, and how people succeed and grow; that is, resiliency.

In this ebook you will learn to move your focus away from pessimism and instead focus on the positive strengths in your relationship in order to deal with the new stressors you each are facing. Did you know that, even while traditional mental health has gone its own stubborn, negative way, a few sociologists and psychologists have been exploring why some people are successful no matter how distressing their life circumstances? They have found not only do some people succeed where others do not, but also they *grow* from their challenging experiences.

"Like a Timex, these folks take a licking and keep on ticking --
and morph into a Rolex!"

In the early stages of the research on resiliency, the answers scientists found were overly simplistic. Psychologists, with their focus on personality, uncovered *traits* that these resilient individuals possessed. Sociologists correctly observed that these personal traits were not particularly helpful if these individuals did not find resources in the world around them. You probably recognize, as we do, that *both are required.* In your relationship you have certain traits, attitudes, and talents in common with your partner and others that are different. The way that your personal qualities fit together gives your relationship your *unique "Power of Two".* However, we all recognize that each relationship is situated in a communal setting that not only serves up challenges but ideally also has some resources you might want to discover and use.

In resilient couples the members:

- Know, respect, and like each other and see themselves as a positive "We".
- Have clear and reasonable goals that organize their lives, and consistently think carefully about how best to pursue them in an efficient and organized fashion.
- Realistically believe in themselves, based on past success, and understand that "luck" is less important than what they do to increase the probability of desirable things happening.

How To Use This Book

Do not try to do everything at once. You don't have to put your entire relationship "under construction". This ebook has an itinerary for how to immediately shift your relationship to become more resilient. Just like on any journey, we have an itinerary with specific steps. This ebook is the map for your journey to resiliency. FIRST USE THE RELATIONSHIP RESILIENCY SURVEY and uncover what for the TWO OF YOU are your best relationship strengths, and what -- relative to them -- are not quite so strong. Later, once your heads and hearts are in a good place, you can see what you want to do to enhance the less strong traits. Once you and — ideally — your partner have assessed your relationship resiliency, you will get immediate feedback through email.

Two copies are given. Some couples like to complete one survey together, but most folks have found that by doing it separately and privately — and then comparing their two surveys, and discovering the differences — they create a richer experience for themselves.

Partner 1

Cluster	Characteristic	Most Like us		?		Least Like us	Cluster Total
Cohesion	1. When together, we are relaxed and comfortable with each other	5	4	3	2	1	
	2. We respect each other's traits including behaviors, reliability, and general outlook	5	4	3	2	1	
	3. We feel included and heard when important decisions are made	5	4	3	2	1	
	4. When things go bad, we find find a way to forgive each other	5	4	3	2	1	
	5. We are committed to making our relationship work	5	4	3	2	1	
Organized adaptive approach	6. When there is a job to be done, we know what our respective duties are	5	4	3	2	1	
	7. Our relationship goals are kept very clear	5	4	3	2	1	
	8. We seek mutual understanding about problems, goals and approaches	5	4	3	2	1	
	9. We are open to flexibility and novel approaches if required	5	4	3	2	1	
	10. We will seek outside help when we need it	5	4	3	2	1	
Problem-solving communication	11. In serious discussions we are able to stay focused on issues	5	4	3	2	1	
	12. We talk to each other in supportive and calming ways	5	4	3	2	1	
	13. We are good at cooling down arguments	5	4	3	2	1	
	14. We are able to express ourselves clearly	5	4	3	2	1	
	15. We are concerned with having all the facts before acting	5	4	3	2	1	
Affirming belief systems	16. We have a high level of commitment to our relationship's well-being	5	4	3	2	1	
	17. We are confident that we will stay together no matter what	5	4	3	2	1	
	18. We share the same world view and belief system	5	4	3	2	1	
	19. We tend to interpret each other's motivations in a positive way	5	4	3	2	1	
	20. We believe our decisions and hard work determine our relationship's success more than luck	5	4	3	2	1	
Emotional Bank Account	21. We admire each other	5	4	3	2	1	
	22. We know how to have fun together	5	4	3	2	1	
	23. We can easily think of good times when we accomplished things together	5	4	3	2	1	
	24. We have had our struggles but agree that it was worth it	5	4	3	2	1	
	25. We are proud of what we have accomplished together	5	4	3	2	1	

Partner 2

Cluster	Characteristic	Most Like us		?		Least Like us	Cluster Total
Cohesion	1. When together, we are relaxed and comfortable with each other	5	4	3	2	1	
	2. We respect each other's traits including behaviors, reliability, and general outlook	5	4	3	2	1	
	3. We feel included and heard when important decisions are made	5	4	3	2	1	
	4. When things go bad, we find find a way to forgive each other	5	4	3	2	1	
	5. We are committed to making our relationship work	5	4	3	2	1	
Organized adaptive approach	6. When there is a job to be done, we know what our respective duties are	5	4	3	2	1	
	7. Our relationship goals are kept very clear	5	4	3	2	1	
	8. We seek mutual understanding about problems, goals and approaches	5	4	3	2	1	
	9. We are open to flexibility and novel approaches if required	5	4	3	2	1	
	10. We will seek outside help when we need it	5	4	3	2	1	
Problem-solving communication	11. In serious discussions we are able to stay focused on issues	5	4	3	2	1	
	12. We talk to each other in supportive and calming ways	5	4	3	2	1	
	13. We are good at cooling down arguments	5	4	3	2	1	
	14. We are able to express ourselves clearly	5	4	3	2	1	
	15. We are concerned with having all the facts before acting	5	4	3	2	1	
Affirming belief systems	16. We have a high level of commitment to our relationship's well-being	5	4	3	2	1	
	17. We are confident that we will stay together no matter what	5	4	3	2	1	
	18. We share the same world view and belief system	5	4	3	2	1	
	19. We tend to interpret each other's motivations in a positive way	5	4	3	2	1	
	20. We believe our decisions and hard work determine our relationship's success more than luck	5	4	3	2	1	
Emotional Bank Account	21. We admire each other	5	4	3	2	1	
	22. We know how to have fun together	5	4	3	2	1	
	23. We can easily think of good times when we accomplished things together	5	4	3	2	1	
	24. We have had our struggles but agree that it was worth it	5	4	3	2	1	
	25. We are proud of what we have accomplished together	5	4	3	2	1	

NEXT

You may want to print out, not only your Resiliency Scale feedback, but also this book. Some of you might save it to your mobile devices. But put these materials in a place where they will catch your attention. Then be sure to look through the pages and topics and, where something strikes your fancy, highlight it and perhaps set aside some time to experiment with some piece of it.

Just as you were advised in your feedback from the Relationship Resiliency Assessment, begin with the areas of your greatest strengths, and do our suggested exercises to remind yourselves of ways in which you already *are* successful and which have given you both pleasure and confidence. Then do more of them. Don't pursue negatives; they will just get in the way. If a negative keeps intruding, convert it into a positive: Ask yourselves "What would we like to be happening instead?"

Do not go after your weakest traits until much later. The best time is when you have thoroughly explored your strongest traits and therefore have solid, realistic, good-feeling about yourselves. *That's* the mood you use to experiment with other things.

In a Nutshell: Our Core Message

Most of us spend too much energy focussing on weaknesses and how to improve them. We are capable of much greater change if we can discover our strengths instead and learn how to bring them to bear in facing life's challenges. Resilient couples do this every day and so can you.

Chapter 1

Preserving and Enhancing our "We-ness" (Cohesion)

One very important characteristic that makes your relationship able to with-stand stress -- and even to grow from It -- Is the extent to which the two of you feel a sense of "we-ness" characterized by mutual respect, loyalty, and mutual goals.

Because of the importance of this characteristic the *Relationship Resiliency Survey* asked you to consider the relative strengths of a number of related examples of it. Some of these were:

• "When together, we are relaxed, comfortable with each other"
• "We have a clear sense of who "we" are, and "our way of doing things""
• "We respect each other's traits including behaviors, reliability, and general outlook"
• "Both of us feel included and heard when important decisions are made"
• "We are committed to making our relationship work"
• "We share the same goals and dreams for our relationship"

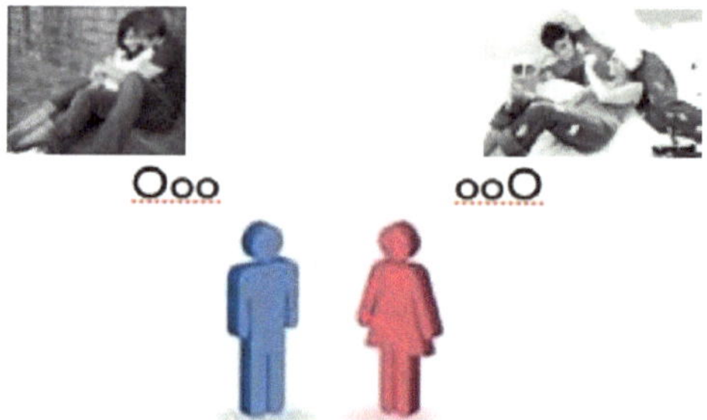

Take a look at each of the above items and talk to each other about which of them you already have at a high level. (Remember, there were a lot of them and we only let you put 5 items in each stack. So there is no way all of them could have been in your highest group!) Then share what it is that you do together that is evidence for the item you are looking at. Then agree on how you can continue to do this, and even do more of it!

Perhaps these recommendations can help you both with this task:

1. Start with the item listed above that you two agree is the strongest in your current relationship.
2. Each of you close your eyes and picture an event in the past few weeks that really — for you — shows that trait in operation. Enjoy that scene. Then: In it, what are you doing? What is your partner doing?
3. Share your observations with each other.

4. Together, think about how you can continue to co-create such events.

   We recommend that you spend most of your attention, time, and energy on these things that are going well or acceptably so. That will increase your sense of well-being and realistic confidence. It will make you happy and secure.

However...

   Sometimes both of you will be in a mood so positive that you will want to consider things you can improve. Only then, consider which of those items listed above are not as strong as some of the others or where the two of you have substantially different opinions, that is, one of you sees an area as higher than does your partner.

1. Each of you think of times in the past few weeks when you thought the trait in question was present.

2. Share your two images.

3. If one of you cannot think of such a positive event, think of an event where it could have been present but, in your opinion, wasn't. Do not focus on the "wasn't". Picture the event and ask yourself and your partner what each of you would have liked to be doing instead. What would you be doing? What would your partner be doing?

4. And,as a result of that, what do the two of you imagine you would have been feeling and thinking?

Catastrophic thinking... How realistic is it?

Are there times when you or your partner do not talk about something that may be important? Rather than obsess over that in the privacy of your own mind, why not ask yourself: "What do I imagine happening if I were to discuss this with my partner?" If you sit quietly and just wait as that question percolates in your mind, a series of ideas will gradually come to you. When these feared consequences are in front of you, ask yourself: "What evidence do I have for that?" "Does this really describe my partner?" "Would I even be with someone like that?"

Typically all of us have "baggage," that is, expectations based on past or present hurt attached to the behavior of important people in our lives, and expected of and perceived in the person in front of us. Our minds protect us in this way: Because of THAT we expect or perceive THIS. So we don't give these new people a chance. For example, say that your employer is a deficit-detective; highly critical, only focussed on perceived shortcomings and mistakes in you, and dismissive of any attempts you make to defend yourself. Would you not eventually come to expect this and see it in your partner? A friend might then ask you: "What evidence do you have that your partner is like that? Has your partner ever done that? In fact, would your employer have listened to you, worried over you, and hugged you?"

"Most modern couples need to create a space for their relationship."

Living together is so much more different than dating. Dating is time set aside to enjoy each other. However, once you live together, that time -- recreational, playing together -- probably has disappeared. Instead, you need to handle life together. Although theologians like to talk about "Life after death," you probably are more immediately concerned with "life after birth". We can predict two separate scenarios:

A. No children; you both are employed outside of your home. Now, how does your day go? Probably the first 10 hours involve time going to and from work and being there. Let's assume that you do not bring your work home with you. So, once home, the next chunk of your time is spent taking care of your basic human maintenance needs, such as laundry, shopping, cooking, eating, and essential clean up. All of these are nonnegotiable. You're stuck with them. Maybe you have a pet or two. That's more non negotiable daily maintenance. We are guessing that you got home by 6 PM and have finished with these fixed requirements of life by, say, 9 PM. So far you have had no real alone-time or quality shared-time. Depending on when you have to get up, how tired you are, and what other obligations and preoccupations you have, the time between 9 PM and midnight is "yours". Most folks, feeling tired and uncreative, fall into a chair and then into bed. Their weekends often involve more of the same life maintenance activities tucked into the maintenance of outside the home personal activities and relationships. Examples would be social obligations, especially those with your individual families.

B. Homes with children. Again, the first 10 hours of your day involve time going to and from work and being there. Daycare drop-off and pick-up may add to this time. Once home, the next chunk of your time is spent taking care of the basic social and survival needs of your children (e.g., parent time, bathing, feeding, settling down). All of this may be complicated by a pet or two. In any case, your own adult survival needs typically have to come after that. There is the laundry, shopping, adult cooking and eating, and essential clean up. All of this is nonnegotiable. It must be done on a daily basis and the structure of most of it is inflexible. Given the non negotiable, survival needs of your children, we are now setting your discretionary time for after 10 or 11 PM. This may or may not go to your relationship! Most of you simply fall into bed.

This "life after birth" reality is far more common than the public suspects. We know that many couples are pregnant before or soon after moving in together. This means that before they have worked out the changes in their lives caused by moving out of a recreational relationship into a living-together one, they also are expectant parents. *Now, think of all the changes that might be involved in moving from lovers, to partners, to expectant parents.* And, within a few months the child has been born and your relationship has moved from being centered on the two of you to being child-centered. As one scientist noted, there is no power greater than that of an infant. Without your constant care, your baby will die.

Of course, some couples may not have had had even a minimal time to get used to these relationship changes. Many of you may have been single parents to begin with. You may have had meager relationship time from the beginning and no time to prepare for what was coming!

An experiment!

Make an appointment with your partner to take three 90-minute walks together in the next two weeks. Walks don't cost money, they provide a sense of companionship, and they are conducive to quiet companionship or easy conversation.

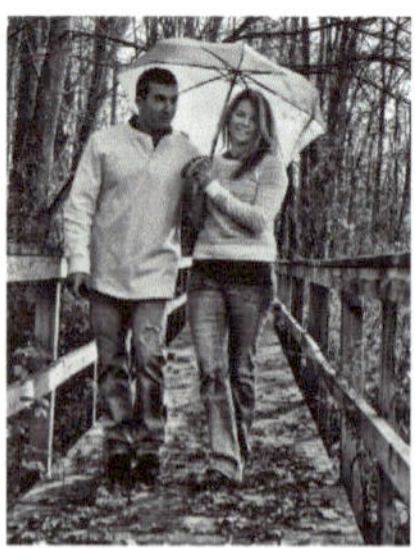

- If you are successful in having all of these walks, all three of them, congratulations to you! Try to keep that going.
- If you have trouble making the appointments, which is more likely, pay attention to what is keeping that from happening for each of you. (Phone calls, work requirements, child-rearing duties, home responsibilities....)
- If you are able to make the appointments, but cannot carry out one or more of them, appreciate together what got in your way.

If you do this exercise, you will either have enjoyable time together or you will get a detailed look at how life conspires against you. (There's no sense in blaming each other.) There are two messages here and they apply to all of us:

1. The problem isn't in your relationship! These increasing complications and their conflict with your quality time together are universal and predictable. *They happen to everyone.* Even if you remain childless, they cannot be avoided. But, if you expect them, you will not be taken by surprise. And, if lucky you have lots of money, you may be able to minimize them if you want to.

2. Since these complications are universal and predictable, beyond not blaming yourselves, you may be able to position yourselves to minimize disruption and to increase the probability of good things happening. If you appreciate your situation in all of its complexity, you can get angry at your life but not necessarily at each other. You can vent to each other without either of you feeling blamed. Ideally you can find and commit to activities that will give you respite from your daily activities, good family time, and something to which to look forward. These can be as simple as participation in a church congregation, scheduled athletic endeavor (such as an athletic league that accommodates both members on a team), or....? As children become older, their parents have come to look forward to their shared deli sandwiches in the bleachers while their children play soccer, T-ball, or softball. Finally, if you are fortunate enough to have family near-by, respite care may be arranged (e.g., date nights wherein the grandparents babysit or host an over-nighter). *Unhappily many couples find themselves isolated from their families and this is where networking with others in similar circumstances can be very vital.*

Resiliency requires alertness for and openness to resources outside of your relationship. However, this also means that:

- The resources have to be out there
- You have to know about them (or create them)
- You have to see them as something you need and want, and
- They have to be in a form that you can use them

Research has discovered that most people experience the most support when they are networked with others in the same circumstances. They remind each other that they all are quite normal, provide each other emotional -- and sometimes concrete -- support, and share ways they have discovered of making things "work". These support groups are formed out of work, school, church, and neighborhood settings.

Note: *Therapists typically focus the things that people say are bothering them and don't challenge their point of view. So they are most likely to think of "problems" as existing in dysfunctional individuals in, perhaps, dysfunctional relationships. As you can tell from our materials, we believe that in many cases this kind of thinking can lead everyone astray. They lead to negative interpretations of ourselves and others. They sap our self esteem and make us pessimistic. Instead, we want you to pay attention to how life works: People typically do well. Then their lives change when some new piece is added. They then find a way of coping with these new features. Let's agree to "Keep It Simple, Logical, and Constructive." See alsoChapter 4, "Affirming Belief Systems".*

Chapter 2

Preserving and Enhancing our Problem-Solving Communication

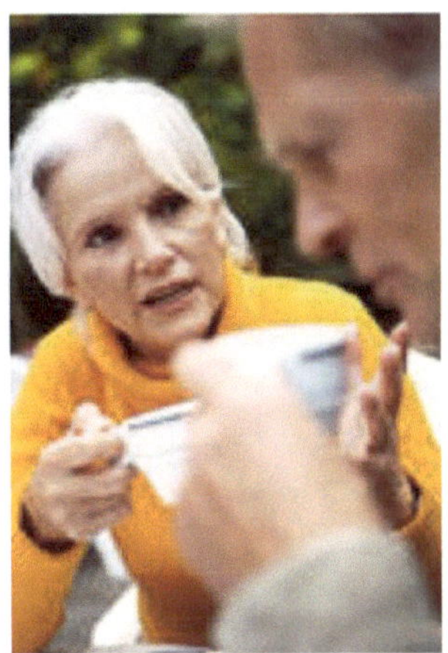

"Positive Conflict" is not a contradictory concept. It is a GOOD thing!

None of us lives in Relationship La-La Land where everything is always peaceful. Let's be real: Do we know of ANY real life couple relationship wherein there is no disagreement, disappointment, or hurt? Positive Psychology research has three things to say about that:

1. First, every relationship is an argument for its own existence. Unless there is partner abuse, you don't have to defend your relationship to anyone; e.g., family, friends, or community. Discover the power of "No," "MYOB," and caller ID.

2. Second, intense fights are signs of a vital relationship. Getting really upset is proof that you are not indifferent to what each other thinks, feels, and does.*

* Partner abuse can be emotional, physical, verbal, sexual, and combinations of these. Intimidation also qualifies. It doesn't matter who started what. Whenever your interactions become abusive, you each need to get to a separate, physically safe place and then, if you wish, work on things at a distance — ideally with a professional facilitator. [http://www.thehotline.org/, 1-800-799-SAFE]

3. Fighting, when you air grievances, is a constructive thing. It is how you get to really know one another and feel safe enough to open up your real selves to each other. And to enjoy the intense relief, security, and joy of being accepted and loved for who you are. How COOL is THAT!

At issue is how you *resolve your complaints*. You have three crucial tools.

A. You don't attempt to discuss things when the two of you are really upset. Instead, you agree to discuss the matter much later in the day when you both are calmer. And then you keep this appointment. (Otherwise why would either of you be willing to let go of the matter when it first came up?)

B. When you do address the grievance, each of you listens, and asks respectful clarifying questions. "From your reaction I could see that you were very upset. What made this so tough on you? I don't want to do more of that!") Neither of you criticizes, shows contempt, or shuts out your partner emotionally. Even if you do not agree at that time, you nevertheless want to send the message that your partner is of the utmost importance to you and you do want to understand.

C. Even though the two of you are constructively pursuing things that are barriers to comfort and problem solving, you both never lose sight of the bigger picture: The "ups" that you bring to each other and create together. Therefore, we would suggest that each of you remember the following mantra: "In the past few weeks, when I and my partner were feeling good about (content with, happy in) our relationship, what was I doing — and what was my partner doing?" It may be that one of these constructive barrier-addressing sessions will become one of those highlights!

The thing is in a relationship, no partner can speak of things honestly and in an emotionally vulnerable way, or set reasonable limits, when either party is highly angry, frightened, or feels beaten down. The safety of each of you must be your first concern. And, if there are children in the home, their safety is paramount as well. Viewing adult abuse, and living with the tension associated with that, does serious short- and long-term damage to them.

One very important characteristic that makes your relationship able to withstand stress -- and even to grow from it -- is the extent to which the two of you have a good-enough plan for problem-solving. This is not a "communication thing". It involves shared goals ("We-ness") that are reasonable and have enough of a working relationship to get the job done.

Don't Forget: Confusion and Disagreement are Good Things! 

When you are confused it means that you intelligent enough to see the complexities of life. People talk about "good" decisions and "bad" decisions. A "good" one leads to your fondest dreams coming true. A "bad" one leads to catastrophe; the end of your good life — forever. Therefore, faced with a decision to be made, their anxiety is at a peak. And who can think creatively at a time like that? Often such people are immobilized or do something impulsively just to get it done. That's not a good way to try to solve problems and to make decisions.

However, you know better than that. You and your partner have *wisdom*. Your corporate wisdom tells you that although luck plays a role in life, your own motives and actions make a significant difference in what befalls you. To some extent people make their own luck. We know a person who was bemoaning a day of terrible misfortune: His teeth were abscessed and most of them would need to be removed; He was terrified of dentists. He also was about to be laid off at the warehouse where he had been employed for ten years. He had just been informed by the Friend of the Court that, if he did not pay $22,000 in back child support, he would be jailed. An onlooker opined that this poor soul had set the stage for such huge misfortune all by himself: He had dropped out of high school, limiting his employment opportunities. Afraid of dentists, he had not taken routine care (if any) of his teeth. He had not paid his child support and had ignored previous warnings by the Friend of the Court. If the man had operated more prudently, it is less likely that this horrible day would have arrived — at least at such a level.

If truth be known, couples cannot guarantee consistent good fortune. However, their common goal would be to do things in such a way that they maximized the probability of desirable things happening. And in such a way that they minimize the probability of undesirable things happening. These are reasonable goals. They are prudent. They are the touchstones to be applied to any decision-making process. *"To what extent will what we are considering increase the likelihood of what we ultimately want?"*

As you can see, two things are necessary for productive decision-making and problem solving:
1. Realistic goals
2. A relationship climate that exploits the benefit of two interdependent parties working together. That is, empowerment because both of you are fully bringing your insights, concerns, and emotional support to the task at hand.

Each of these will be elaborated later. First, however, you will want to look at how the two saw yourselves generally in this regard on the *Relationship Resiliency Survey.*

Your Self-Assessment of Your Problem-solving Resources

The *Relationship Resiliency Survey* asked you to think about many examples of problem solving resources shown by the two of you. Some of them recognized how you keep each other calm and thoughtful. Others appreciated how you use each other as problem-solving resources; how "two heads are better than one". Some described your flexibility, and so on. A few of these examples are listed here:

- *"In serious discussions we are able to stay focused on issues "*
- *"We talk to each other in supportive and calming ways"*
- *"We seek input from each other"*

- *"We are open to criticism"*
- *"Our disagreements help us get a broader view of things"*
- *"We tend to seek mutual understanding and consensus"*
- *"We can change our way of doing things if conditions require it "*
- *"We are concerned with having all the facts before acting"*

Take a look at each of these examples and talk to each other about which of them you already have at a high level. (Remember, since we only let you put 5 items in each stack, *there is no way all of them could have been in your highest group!*) Then share what it is that you do together that is evidence for the item you are looking at. Then agree on how you can *continue to do this, and even do more of it!*

Perhaps these recommendations can help you both with this task:

1. Start with the item listed above that you two agree is the strongest in your current relationship.
2. Each of you close your eyes and picture an event in the past few weeks that really — for *you* — shows that trait in operation. Enjoy that scene. Then: In it, w*hat are you doing? What is your partner doing?*
3. Share your observations with each other.
4. Together, think about how you can continue to co-create such events.
5. If you wish, look at where you had different impressions of something as a resource, and explore each other's differing perspective.

The Importance of Shared Goals

Decisions and problem solving are less difficult the two of you have a robust sense of "We-ness" based on shared goals. Shared goals not only enhance your sense of who-you-are-together, they also anchor you to a common foundation of belief and values, while giving you a framework for making decisions.

Laying the Groundwork for Your Lives Together. Keeping it clear, reasonable, and simple.

Keeping it Clear and Reasonable

Happily, you two have already agreed to operate on the general principle of doing things in the here-and-now that increase the probability of desirable short- and long-term outcomes. Problem-solving gurus observe that these actions also should be:
- **Realistic.** They actually can be accomplished over the long term.

- ***Under your control.*** They largely can be done by you. Your goals are not in the hands of chance or reliant upon unpredictable other people and institutions.
- ***Observable.*** Your behaviors and their short-term outcomes should be defined as tangible actions that both of you can see, track, and evaluate.
- ***Positive.*** Goals should be stated as positive actions. Rather than thinking of what you do not want to do (focusing on buzz-killers), focus on what you would like to be doing *instead*.

Keeping it Simple: ." The number three +/- two"

Back in the 1960s, researchers tried to ascertain how many things a person could handle at any one time. For air traffic controllers they arrived at seven airplanes, plus or minus two. So! Think of how many things you are trying to keep track of in your life; how many balls you are juggling all of the time. Your lives together might be less urgent if you had only three or four mutual, relatively non-negotiable aspirations for you and yours.

Why not give yourselves this much-needed relief? Sit down together and select three or four things you want for yourselves, now and ultimately, more than *anything else*. They may be life values (being tranquil, being best friends, seeking adventure, etc.) or tangible outcomes (financial security, higher social status, accomplished children, and so on). *Whatever. It will be the uniquely you.*

1.
2.
3.
4.

Now, think of other goals you and people around you have for you. You might want to write them down. However, the main thing is to *let go of everything else* -- or at least move then into a much lower position. Hanging onto them, keeping track, and pursuing them at your highest energy levels will be too much work. Use only your Big Four goals to dictate decisions you make: *"Will our decision increase the probability of one or more of these Big Four happening?"*

Common Barriers to Decision-making

A Clash of What Each of You Wants First

Do you get frustrated with your partner when you have something on your mind? A common blind spot -- your individual adaptive styles -- may be getting in your way.

Hearing a problem, some of us are "Fixers". When a problem is brought up, some of us immediately see a need to FIX IT. That's how they see themselves being useful and what they expect their partners want from them.

Others ("Communicators") are not looking for solutions to the problem — they just want to TALK ABOUT IT. They do not want relief by "solving the problem"; they want the comfort that comes from empathic listening. Self esteem, security, and solace come from networking.

When one of each type -- once thought to characterize traditional male and female roles -- is in the same relationship, both parties predictably spend a lot of time being frustrated and perplexed!

This unrecognized conflict in coping styles can spiral into substantial relationship distancing. In best case scenarios, the one who needs a listener will find someone else to talk to, and the Fixer will draw false comfort from the silence. In a worst case scenario, one frustrated partner stubbornly keeps trying to get the other to "fix" things and concludes that the partner doesn't really want to. And the partner is losing faith and composure because all that person is looking for is empathic companionship.

Relationship lesson: When it seems like one or both of you are feeling the impossibility of things, each ask your partner what you would like from the other at this particular time -- one who empathically listens or a concrete solution to the other's concern? *Take care of your relationship first. Everything else is secondary.*

Thinking in Terms of Extremes

To what extent are you looking for unrealistic solutions because you are thinking of "right" or "wrong," or "good" or "bad" decisions. In life, when one chooses a course of action a path unfolds are a result of that action. That journey will be to some degree different than if you picked another path. No one can say which would have been better over time; they were different journeys leading to different life experiences. Good-enough, better, and other evaluative judgment only make sense with regard to some specific criteria. "Better" for accomplishing *what*? We have suggested the extent to which a chosen course of action increases the probability of what — for the two of you — are desirable things occurring.

Catastrophic Thinking

It is always profitable to explore how realistic your immediate and long-term fears are. *"What do I imagine happening if we were to do this?"* If you both sit quietly and just wait as that question percolates in your minds, a series of ideas will gradually come to you. When these feared consequences are in front of you, ask yourselves: "What evidence do we have for that?" "Are other outcomes possible?"

A Sense of "Impossibility"

Some experts say that some things are beyond a person's control. For example, a noted research recently claimed that parents had little influence on their children's lives; their children's peer groups had a much larger shaping influence. What an uncreative, non-insightful conclusion! First of all, the values and opportunities parents give to their children will influence who later will be influential peers. They cannot pick the exact friends their children will have, but they certainly can select the pools from which their children will find them. They do this by picking certain neighborhoods in which to live, certain schools with which to become actively involved, and certain institutions, groups, and activities to expose their offspring. *For example, one couple had their daughter learn to play a wind instrument in the third grade, knowing there was a high likelihood that she would thence forward be a member of school orchestras and marching bands, and hence surrounded by academically-oriented late-bloomers.* How does this kind of strategizing fit the things you care about.

Parental Legacies

Often our parents and first families shape how we later do things in our lives. One expert theorized that parents take care of their children and then are paid back by those children raising their children the way that the parents raised them. It is your way of telling your parents that they did the "right thing". And usually your parents need to hear that affirmation. But what happens when you and your partner decide to remain childless or, having children, indulge them in certain ways? What if you decide to privilege career over home, or vice versa? What if you and your partner relate in ways in which either sets of parents did not?

When we do, prioritize, or decide things other than our parents would have done it, we usually are very aware of it. It is as if they suddenly are looking over our shoulders. We feel a tension. The expert would say that when you do such a thing your parents feel accused. We may deny that intent, observing quite reasonably that they chose their lives, under unique circumstances, as we now choose ours. Still we feel the tension! When that happens, remember the probable source, reaffirm your own values and plans of action, and keep on doing! This is your "We-ness" looking for empowerment.

Chapter 3

Creating and Maintaining an Organized Adaptive
Approach

"Growing Stronger, Together"

Being able to communicate effectively is drop-dead wonderful. But it may not be enough. You need to be *on the same page*, both in terms of what you want, and how you intend to work together to obtain goals and overcome what you two perceive to be challenges to your corporate well-being.

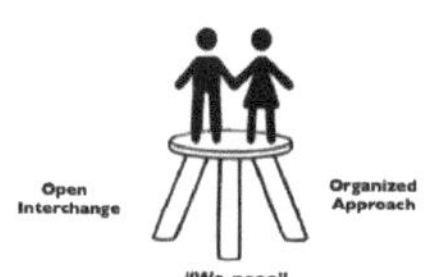

This stool is held up by three legs. Remove one, and it falls. And it only is as stable as the strength of its weakest leg. All three legs must be strong and united in their contribution. One of those legs is being able to talk to and explore one another's experience and ideas. Another one is "We-ness" -- seeing yourselves as a problem-solving task force and being on the same page in terms of what you want for your corporate selves. The third leg is an *organized and effective way of using your resources to overcome challenges and get what you both want.*

Why You Need an Organized Approach:

Chaos is not just a theory; It is a fact of life

Some Facts of Life are really Facts of *Living*. One of the more important is that, by virtue of just being alive, you will face continual challenges. However, unlike sickness, accidents, and such some challenges will be predictable; they are universal and unavoidable. And they will totally disrupt your lives. That's why "Being a Couple" is a good thing! It is a problem-solving relationship. However, in coupling you have set yourselves up for a series of disruptive challenges. Consider:

Upon adulthood, each of you moved toward self-sufficiency. You needed to get a residence, finance and manage your individual day-to-day lives. You had to work your way free of problematic family entanglements and get comfortable in your own skins. You found out how to establish and maintain adult peer relationships. You then agreed with someone to become exclusive lovers. You probably floundered about in each of these novel situations, but eventually got comfortable.

Then you probably moved in with each other. You both discovered that this was a "hot mess" that required a lot of attention. At the very least:

- You had to transition from a recreational relationship to a problem-solving one.

- You had to figure out how to live together, with each other's habits, values, and eccentricities.

- You had to come up with a domestic division of labor; who is expected to do what, when.

- You had to figure out how to manage others friends, work, and — probably — families.

- And, if there were children involved, you had to move from you and relationship being the center of your universe; it is now a child-centered one.

And (applause!) *the two of you have done all of that. While also managing your occupational lives.* That's a lot of work; not too shabby! Or you still working at these, which all new couples must do. And you now have affirmation of all the craziness you have had to sort out!

But Life being what it is, there's always going to be a ziggy: Each time you and your partner have adjusted and are doing good enough, you are eventually going to hit an invisible wall. You again will feel frustrated and confused. But being made of hardy stuff you will try-try again. *Nada.* However, as we have often heard "one definition of 'insanity' is doing the same thing over and over again and expecting things to turn out differently." "You can't win using your tried-and-true methods because you are facing new circumstances that require new tools!

The Biggest Picture is this: You are cruising along and doing well. Then your life circumstances change, and your old ways of doing thing don't fit. There is a period of discomfort. Then you find and employ new ways to fit the new circumstances and you cruise along — until your life circumstances change again. These changes will occur; No amount of planning can avoid them. They come from being alive in our society.

The good news is that the benefits of coupledom outweigh the challenges, and you have a partner to help you figure out how to handle them. The bad news is that, in coping, no specific techniques will work all the time. You need an *organized plan* for approaching challenges and solving them.

"How Organized Are We in Our Approach to Coping and Planning?"

The importance of that third leg is why you were asked to consider examples of it from your relationship. Some of the items involved were:

- "We encourage each other to work together"
- "We are in agreement about the role each of us should play in our real relationship"
- "Our goals for ourselves are kept very clear"
- "We are clear about how tasks are best accomplished"
- "We don't let other family members push us apart"
- "We seek mutual understanding about problems, goals and approaches"
- "We don't let conflict get out of hand"
- "We feel safe in our dealings with each other"
- "We get outside help when we need it"

These kinds of items explore the following characteristics of your relationship: The relative strengths of your "we-ness," your knowledge of what you want for yourselves as a couple, and your organization for how you intend to work together... both in terms of what you expect each other to do, and having a climate that facilitates sharing of challenges.

Take a look at each characteristic and talk to each other about those characteristics you already have at a high level. (Remember, since we only let you put 5 items in each stack, *there is no way all of them could have been in your highest group!*) Then share what it is that you do together that is evidence for the item you are looking at. Then agree on how you can continue to do this, and even do more of it!

Perhaps these recommendations can help you both with this task:

1. Start with the item listed above that you two agree is the strongest in your current relationship.
2. Each of you close your eyes and picture an event in the past few weeks that really — for *you* — shows that trait in operation. Enjoy that scene. Then: In it, *what are you doing? What is your partner doing?*
3. Share your observations with each other.
4. Together, think about how you can continue to co-create such events.
5. If you get stuck on a negative image, ask yourselves what you would like to be doing *instead*.

As always, we recommend that you spend most of your attention, time, and energy on these things that are going well or acceptably so. That will increase your sense of well-being and realistic confidence. It will make you happy and secure while giving the two of you a template for handling challenges now and in your future together.

Solidifying Your Foundation: An Invitation to Learn More about Yourselves

Once a relationship moves away from being strictly recreational, and you are thinking of handling the affairs of life together, its purpose moves beyond fun and personal enrichment. Your relationship now concerns problem-solving and planning. In doing this, the two of you need to work out what your jobs are. You each need to appreciate what you expect of yourselves and what you expect of your partner. Some of these are obvious to both of you and you can talk about them openly, for example "fidelity": *"While we are together neither of us will have an affair of the heart or the body with anyone else; This includes 'fishing' on the internet and solitary pornography."* Notice how this couple uses a label ("faithfulness"), but then goes on to specify what behaviors are and are not an example. Not all expectations are so clear. Often some of the most influential are not! Some of them are unstated and you and your partner may even be *unaware of them.* They come from growing up in a certain family and community, and also from past experiences from your individual lives. Based on "who each of you are" you have basic expectations about your own responsibilities in a relationship. You also have expectations of what your partner should contribute.

Instructions. Each of you take a piece of notebook paper; a big one. Fold it in half length-wise. At the top of the first half (lavender in the illustration below) write "Things I expect from being in this relationship". Then, without looking at each other's page, write down all the things that come to your mind. Take your time, and only quit when you both have run out of ideas. Please, it is important that you each be **very specific about what you put in your list.** General words like "friendship," "loving" or "sharing" are too vague -- Instead put down what friends do, that is, what YOU see as being friends; in your mind what "loving" and "sharing" consist of. When you are done, go to the inside (blue) half and write at the top "Things I ought to provide in this relationship". Again, each of you in private, make your list.

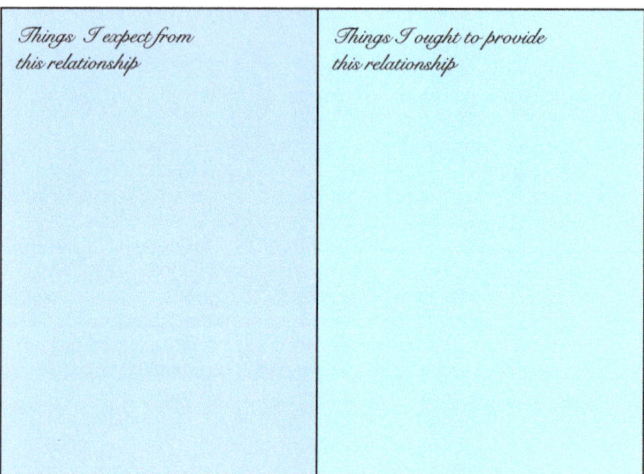

You will wind up with each of you having a **personal relationship contrac**t. What it says is: "If I do THIS (green list), I ought to get THAT (blue list). You probably will discover some surprises and they will make a lot of things now make sense!

For example:

(1) Put your lavender list (what you are looking to get) together with your partner's blue one (what your partner sees as his or her obligations). How much agreement is there?
(2) Now, put your blue list (what you see as things you owe your relationship) next to your partner's green list (what your partner expects to get from your relationship)

Now here is where insights incredibly valuable to your relationship come from: Sit side-by-side and make a note of where your two "personal contracts" are not in agreement. *You each have a relationship contract, but are they the same one?*

Unbeknownst to you, after all this time you may have been at cross purposes. *What you want and what your partner wants may not be the same things. In fact, even when the items on your list sound the same -- "loving," "sharing" and so on -- you may define them differently.* For one person "being loved" means respect, considerateness, acceptance. To another it may be communicated by companionship and physical acts of affection.

What is a Couple to Do?

Can you see the irony here? ***Where you are not in agreement, you can be working as hard as you can on the relationship and still be disappointed, or still be disappointing your partner!*** Take a moment to let this notion sink in. Then:
- Sit and think about times when this may have been happening and share what you were thinking and feeling at those times.
- Ask each other what you might do to get make your two individual contracts overlap and be a shared one. (It's possible that just participating in this exercise may have gotten it done!)
- It might be interesting to explore where each person's items came from and therefore that expectation's power. An expectation might come from an unchallenged positive life model, for example, "That's the kind of relatedness I've always seen." Or, perhaps, an item is based on a strong negative life model: "I don't want us to be like that." These insights are jewels.
- When a challenge arises, what do each of you see as your division of labor?

A Word about "Outside Resources"

Relationship resiliency requires recognition of when you are in over your heads and may need outside help. However, if you live in the middle of the desert and also have no internet, you may be stuck. If, however, you are not so isolated, you probably have some resources out there. And that's important. We talk about getting outside help, but:

☑ The help has to actually be there.
☑ One of you has to know it is there.
☑ You both must want it.
☑ It must be in a form that you are able to use it.

For example, let's say that a community has a *"Drop Off Center -- No Questions Asked"* to give some breathing room to parents who are at wits end and need to calm down. For this outside resource to be helpful, stressed-out parents must appreciate their need to take a "time out" and collect themselves. The drop-off center also needs to be safe for their children and available at least from 5 AM to midnight. If there are fees, they need to be low. The parents need to know about the center, have the means to get their children to it, and have enough self esteem and good sense to take advantage of it. Since it is no doubt in a public place, the drop-off center should have a parking lot shielded from public view and also have a positive title, e.g., "Drop in Play Center for Kids". (If its name were "Child Abuse Protective Services," wouldn't most folks have second thoughts about going there?)

Beware "Unholy Alliances"! Sometimes outside help is not always helpful or "worth it". Sometimes its emotional cost outweighs whatever is offered and a couple, while tempted, knows that it may help them over the short run but at a cost -- if not now, in the future -- to their we-ness, autonomy, privacy, and priorities. The outside help, even if free, is just too expensive. Caveat emptor: "Let the buyer beware!"

Chapter 4

Preserving and Enhancing our Affirming Belief Systems

The Biggest Picture

Two hundred years of psychobabble boils down to two "truths". How you *think* about something determines how you *feel* about it. Conversely, your mood (how you *feel*) can shape how you *think* about things. You can grow stronger, together if you and your partner keep these these factoids in mind. They will help you to appreciate each other while increasing your ability to manage your lives.

If you look at things through an optimistic lens, you feel secure and empowered. For example, realizing that you and your partner work well together will predispose you to feel confident in making plans and facing challenges. *If you are in a positive mood, things pretty much look good to you.* On days when you feel good about yourself and/or about your relationship (a "good hair day" emotionally) you feel secure, and maybe even optimistic, about what the day will bring. If, instead, you get up on the wrong side of the bed, you are likely to interpret even trivial happenings in a negative way. And, worse, if your overall philosophical outlook is that life is a crap shoot, and that you and your partner are generally devoid of luck, you will tend to worry over things and try not to expose yourself to what you expect to be risks. (See also Chapter 5.)

Of course, variations in how you feel about life and how you interpret things (including the motivation lying behind your partner's behavior) are commonplace. So you want to keep an eye on your overall orientation toward your partner, other people, and life itself and factor it into your assessments of who you are, what you do, and how successful you might be. The two of you do not want to support false hopes and denial in each other. However, you also won't want to be overly negative in your assessment of your world. Your goal is to determine what life course, for you, is *reasonable* and *prudent*.

You will also want to help each other with regard to specific days and events. You can grow stronger, together, by looking over each other's shoulders and bringing attention to the tone of what is being thought and felt. Are you and/or your partner looking at things through a darkish lens or through a more sunny one? How objective are you being? What are your expectations and attributions? For example, do you expect negativity from that parent or that friend? Does this then color how you interpret a look or a comment? Indeed, sometimes you or your partner may be inclined to remember negative things done by others because in doing so, you feel more we-ness.

So overall, and in specific situations, are you and/or your partner looking through rose-colored lenses, darkish lenses, or something more neutral? It may be important to know that relationship experts have discovered that the quality of your relationship future depends on how you and your partner look at each other; that is, whether you believe that your partner's behavior toward you indicates benign as opposed to negative motives, e.g, "My partner is late because of traffic" vs. "My partner is late because of in-difference to my feelings."

Quickie exploration. Perhaps you can sit quietly together with your partner and think of a recent event wherein one of you saw things more negatively and your partner helped you re-think it. Picture one such event for each of you and see in your mind's eye what you were doing, thinking, and feeling, and what your partner was doing that was helpful. Remember those events and try to do more of them!

Stages of Growth

Your relationship comfort and your coping are easily predicted! Like every-one else, you and your partner do fine until something in your lives change and your old ways of handling things don't work anymore. What happens then? There is a period of confusion and frustration, followed by one of two outcomes:

1. *Empowerment.* The two of you recognize that something novel is happening. There-fore, you remind yourselves to relax and prepare to be flexible. Then together you figure out new ways to meet the new circumstances. This way you grow strong to-

gether — because you are building realistic optimism. Your optimism is realistic because it is anchored in your increasing experience of the power of you two expecting life changes as the normal course of things, and planning and working together.

2. ***Dysfunction.*** The two of you keep stubbornly to your usual ways, hoping that something "out there" will change. Some folks even use a little denial or blame their lack of successful coping on others. These folks bog down and often lose faith in themselves and each other.

Getting Down to Specifics

The items on the *Relationship Resiliency Survey* capture the complex nature of "affirming belief systems". They describe your commitment to your personal and corporate well-being, including how you regard yourselves and each other. The items also describe the extent to which you and your partner use experience to flexibly address challenges. Finally, you also assess the level at which you and your partner feel like you together can influence the affairs of your life. Some examples of the items you sorted are:

"We have a high level of commitment to our relationship's well-being"
"We try to work out what causes problems in our life together and try to learn from them"
"We believe that we can influence/control our destiny"
"We are confident that we will stay together no matter what"
"We believe that changes in our way of doing things will sometimes be necessary"
"We share the same world view and belief system"
"We tend to interpret each other's motivations in a positive way"

Take a look at each characteristic and talk to each other about those characteristics you already have at a high level. (Remember, since we only let you put 5 items in each stack, *there is no way all of them could have been in your highest group!)* Then share what it is that you do together that is evidence for the item you are looking at. Then agree on how you can continue to do this, and even do more of it!

Perhaps these recommendations can help you both with this task:

1. Start with the item listed above that you two agree is the strongest in your current relationship.
2. Each of you close your eyes and picture an event in the past few weeks that really-for *you* — shows that trait in operation. Enjoy that scene. Then: In it, w*hat are you doing? What is your partner doing?*
3. Share your observations with each other.
4. Together, think about how you can continue to co-create such events.
5. If you get stuck on a negative image, ask yourselves what you would like to be doing *instead.*

As always, we recommend that you spend most of your attention, time, and energy on those things that are going well or acceptably so. That will increase your sense of well-being and realistic confidence. It will make you happy and secure while giving the two of you a template for handling challenges now and in your future together.

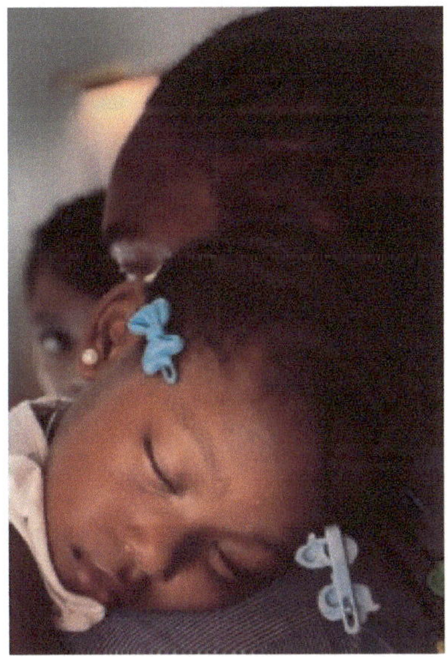

Cultivating Your Process

Management by Objectives

Professional business gurus advise managers -- which is what you are -- not to be solely focused on their here-and-now affairs. Instead they also should be future- oriented. They should decide what business they are in and set up aspirational targets toward which they devote substantial energy. You and your partner are in the "relationship business" and if you intend to cultivate your resiliency, your relationship objectives should include the acquisition of a substantial store of experiences that demonstrate that:

• You are committed to each other and the well-being of both of you (and your relationship)
• You have good-enough (for you) achievements based on the two of you planning and working together
• You appreciate the we-ness that is "Us" as you change in step with your changing world.

☛   If you haven't done it yet, take the time -- *right now* -- to sit down together and select three or four things other than the above you want for yourselves, now and ultimately, more than *anything else.* They may be life values (being tranquil, being best friends, seeking adventure, etc.) or tangible outcomes (financial security, higher social status, accomplished children, and so on). *Whatever. It will be the uniquely you.*

1.

2.

3.

4.

    These goals and the (bulleted) ones urged upon you, should be the focus of all of your planning and the touchstones for your decision-making. *Let everything else go.* Otherwise your mutual burden will be too complex, complicated, conflictual, and heavy. You are stewards of your resources, which includes your energy. You need to make wise choices that allow you to focus on what counts *for you.*

Again, your ultimate goal is to grow stronger, together.

Chapter 5

YOUR RELATIONSHIP INVENTORY: MAKE THE RIGHT INVESTMENTS IN YOUR PORTFOLIO

CEA: "Certified Emotional Accounting"

One social theory suggests that, if the good in a relationship outweighs the bad, people will stay together. This theory answers the ever-popular question of "Why do we put up with each other?" Reply: *"Because the good things we have are more important to us than the bad."*

This accounting concept — while unsentimental — highlights the need for you and your partner to make periodic positive deposits in your joint Emotional Bank Account. This in turn raises the question of "how much is enough?" Needless to say, various relationship gurus have tried to answer that.

Playing the Numbers: What is "enough"?

- One celebrated expert and Friend of Oprah (Dr. John Gottman) sets the ratio at 5:1. *If you are to be a stable and happy couple, every criticism and negative comment should be offset by at least five (5) compliments and positive comments.*

- *A noted business consultant has observed that, at home as in the office, one "Oh, crap" wipes out 10 "attaboys".*

Non-bean counters (these are folks who are not graduates of STEM programs; science, technology, engineering, and mathematics), ignore such formulas and listen to their hearts. They advise you and your partner to *"just keep an eye on things. A reservoir of good feelings will get you through a lot of bad days."*

Don't Discount Your Moods in What You Think You See! The Importance of Checking Your Relationship Goggles

Are there "WTF !??!" moments when one of you gets unexpectedly slammed by your partner? Sometimes AT THE VERY WORST TIME? For example:

At the end of a stressful day you've been held up in maddening traffic, your cell phone is dead, and finally — greatly relieved — you open your door. And see an unwelcoming frown and hear "Where have you BEEN?" You expected a welcoming smile and a sympathetic hug. Instead, your partner is tense, angry, and accusing. "WTF?" is your (internal) response. But if you say it, the remainder of your day will be cold and nasty. You each will feel alienated from the other. And probably this episode will be thrown into your respective gunny sacks of grievances.

Ouch! If you have bought and are reading this book, you are committed to building a healthy and satisfying relationship. So let's unpack the above episode.

- Partner 1 is feeling unjustly beat up at a time when Partner 1 wanted a hug and sympathetic inquiry, perhaps followed by a beer or glass of wine. Or maybe just some unwinding time alone in the bathroom.

· Partner 1 doesn't know that Partner 2 also has had a horrid day, brought work home, and saw a mess upon coming through the door. Nevertheless, Partner 2 has fixed a nice dinner and has been waiting for "inconsiderate and self-serving" Partner 1, who "at least could have called."

Why do our partners react this way? Yes, our partners could have been raised by feral jackals and not have a sensitive or considerate bone in their bodies. More likely, unhelpful belief systems have come into play.

Level 1. Lenses.

"What COLOR are YOUR relationship goggles — most of the time and moment-to-moment?" Are they brown (poo-colored) or are they rose-colored (coated with "we-ness" and belief in your partner's good will)? These goggles determine what you are expecting and what you therefore "see". Then your subsequent behavior toward your partner may follow suit, and perhaps influence your partner to react in sweet or ugly ways.

Level 2. Unhelpful, unvoiced, unchallenged belief systems.

A partner assumes that "THIS means THAT" – THIS means "You don't love me." For example, "If you don't call when you are going to be late, you don't care about me." "If you don't take out the trash, leave the toilet seat down or up, you don't love me." "If you loved me, you would pick up your socks." "If you were thinking about me, you would have thrown some Ben & Jerry's in the shopping cart."

Piffles (PFLs). "Personal Philosophies of life." Room-mates are different from Recreational Lovers. When you live together, how each partner handles the trivia of everyday life suddenly matters. If you live by yourself, who cares where you drop your soiled clothes, if you drink milk out of the bottle, let dishes pile up in the sink, squeeze toothpaste from the middle of the tube, or don't turn out lights when leaving a room (to name a few?)

Your partner might have issue with one or all of those things! Each partner has learned "values," and values have the status of MORAL LAW. A Decent Person pays bills on time, puts soiled clothes in hamper, keeps counters clear, turns out the lights when not using them, and always has toilet paper come over the top of the role (and — note to MY partner -- ALWAYS replaces an empty roll). To do otherwise is a sin against God and Man. And a Sure Sign of having been raised in a barn.

There is an irony here: Often lovers are people who help each other stay calm and even grow in desirable ways: Partner 1 is loved because of a certain relaxed quality characterized by spontaneity, *joi de vivre*, and adventure. This creates a buoyancy that Partner 2 finds liberating and joyous. Partner 2, on the other hand, is expected to bring a more settled and responsible quality to the relationship. However, when each partner does what the other partner hired them to do, what happens? "You're totally irresponsi-ble!" "You are so uptight you squeak!"

Lessons

- Our moods often determine what we expect and therefore how we in-terpret our partners' behavior. If we are in a bad mood, a sympathetic sigh by one's partner instead might be heard as rejection.

- Pre-existing beliefs may shape how we feel and therefore how we be-have. For example, partners may have come to learn "the hard way" from previous relationships with parents and lovers intimacy and inter-dependency are dangerous. They therefore enter new relationships with caution, prudence, and preservation of their senses of self-suffi-ciency.

- Moods and reactions may vary from circumstance to circumstance, or go unchallenged for years. Unhappily negative expectations lead to self-fulfilling prophecies. (We call them "death spirals"!) One expects a negative reaction, and therefore interprets their partner's behavior as being negative. Which probably leads their partner to feel confused and angry ("WTF?!!?"). To which the first partner then reacts, and so on. That's why we call it a "deal spiral" — there typically is an escala-tion or a shutting down.

Whenever this occurs (namely, a WTF-moment, or you experience 100 pounds of dynamite where a few ounces would have been more appropriate), remember the "you" in "we". Partners need to check the color of their goggles. This best occurs after a mu-tually-agreed-upon time out (see Chapter 2).

Self Assessment

Because a reservoir of good feelings about yourselves-in-this-relationship is such an important contributor to the climate in which you live, tolerate, plan, and work togeth-er on goals — and how you perceive outside help — you were asked to consider many examples from your relationship. Some of these examples were:

"We know how to have fun together"
"We can easily think of good times when we accomplished things together"
"We honor each other's beliefs and values"
"We have had our struggles but it's been worth it"
"The good things in our relationship outweigh the bad ones"
"We are proud of what we have accomplished" "We have taken good care of each oth-er"

Take a look at each of the above examples and talk to each other about those characteristics you already have at a high level. (Remember, since you could only put 5 items in each stack, *there is no way all of them could have been in your highest group!*) Then share what it is that you do together that is evidence for the item you are looking at. Finally, agree on how you can continue to do each item, and even do more of it! Perhaps these recommendations can help you both with this task.

As always, we recommend that you spend most of your attention, time, and energy on those things that are going well or acceptably so. That will increase your sense of well-being and realistic confidence. It will make you happy and secure while giving the two of you a template for handling challenges now and in your future together.

If you were to go on a relationship enrichment retreat or consult a relationship counselor, an early goal would be to "warm up" your relationship. In order to resurrect your good feelings and closeness you would be asked to describe how you met, what attracted you to each other, and what sorts of foibles got in the way of the two of you getting together. You might then be asked to revisit some of your good times together, and even some funny ones. Since you are not at a retreat or in a counselor's office, *try the following two exercises at home!*

#1. *Set up —this scene and watch your relationship get a nice jolt!*

Picture yourself engaged in some solo activity — perhaps out in the yard or garage. On the kitchen table is a glass and a bottle of wine or a bucket of beers. A photo album sits alongside. Your partner comes by, sees this arrangement, smiles, and sits down. While sipping the mild alcoholic beverage, your partner opens the album and be-

gins to leaf through it.... You join your partner after a bit, top off your partner's glass, pour one for yourself and, with your hand on your partner's shoulder, cheek-to-cheek, you reminisce together. (There probably is nothing as effective as snapshots of the two of you and yours to bring back overlooked memories and their good feelings.)

2. Contract to Write Three "Like" Letters

Sometimes you need to be in the right mood, and also have the private time to think appreciatively of your relationship. *And* sometimes it is better to put your thoughts and feelings into writing. *And* for your partner to get them at a time when your partner can pay attention to what you are communicating while not having to make an immediate reply; instead, you want each other to think and feel about deeply about the question at hand. Letters are a good way to get this done. Both of you must take some time to be alone to gather your thoughts and write a letter to each other and to react to the one you receive from your partner. Here's the plan: Write one letter to your partner at a time. Then leave it somewhere for your partner to find (in his or her laptop case, lunch bag, sink in the bathroom, etc.). After both of you have spent some private time with each other's letters - Don't rush into it! Give things time to sink in — come together to discuss them.   One letter at a time, write them on the following subjects:

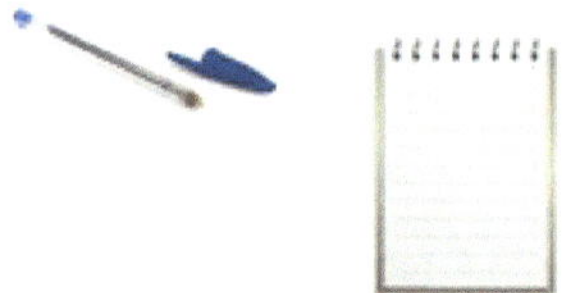

Letter # 1. *"Times in the past few weeks when I just felt happy and content in our relationship"* (perhaps when you just felt loved and/or valued by your partner). What were you doing, what was your partner doing, and what were you thinking and feeling? You might add "Little things we do that I wish we would *do more of*".

Letter # 2. *"Things we have done that have meant a lot to me."*

Letter # 3. *"Things we are doing that mean a lot to me"*

Taking Time Out to Assess Your Inventory of Good Will

Because couples have busy, complex, and compelling daily lives, they find themselves preoccupied with the present with — at best — an eye on the near future. In their need to meet their non-negotiable survival needs, they have tunnel vision that gets in the way of seeing their larger picture.

For example, when the two of you were writing and discussing your letters, to what extent did you remember and credit the "Big Stuff"?

· Think about some of your major joint accomplishments, such as obtaining and setting up your first residence, and working out a way to support each other's aspirations. You may revisit the warm glow you both got from feeling financially secure ($ ka-ching $). If you are older, and have children, perhaps you will consider your quiet satisfaction as you sat in the stands at a t-ball or soccer game and, later, when you attended graduations.

· You probably also can remember times when you defended one another against invasive outsiders: Friends and relatives who were critical and/or who tried to make their opinions your own. They tried to apply pressure about how one of you looked, where you decided to live, what your relationship should be like, when and how to have babies, and so on. But your partner got between them and you, or you both built a protective wall around yourselves and your "we-ness".

· There are times when you decided on scary plans together or took on challenges — and were successful! What might some of those times be?
    ·

Not everything is huge. Sometimes things are small parts of everyday life. They too are important items in your emotional inventory.

For example, many times you and your partner tell each other that you are in love, not by what you say, but what you do. For example, you do things for each other motivated by affectionate consideration, e.g., picking up your partner's special treats at the grocery, arranging for your partner to have some solo quiet time, and sharing a spontaneous hug. Perhaps you clear out some non pressured time for the two of you to sit close on the sofa — without expectations of it "going further". It even may be something so mundane as doing a chore without being asked, for example, taking out the trash or washing your partner's car. Sometimes these non-verbal statements of love take place several times in the course of a day. Your partner sets out coffee for you in the morning, calls at noon to see how your day is going, "just listens" when you need to vent on getting home again, or lets you have time to cool down when you come in from work.

Big events and small, it is important to make positive investments in your relationship portfolio. It also is important to review this portfolio periodically and reflect together on what you both do to make consistent deposits. What you discover will go a long way toward creating a climate in which you can grow stronger, together, forever!

Talk to us.

Send us feedback about your experiences with this eBook!
[Your thoughts, feelings, and examples will influence the next edition.]

relee@fsu.edu; joe@drhorak.com

About the author. Bob Lee has been doing, teaching, researching, and writing about couples and family therapy for 50 years. At mid-life he started educating and training marriage and family therapists, first at Michigan State University, and subsequently at Florida State University. He is Professor Emeritus at the latter.